Look Inside a
Tree

Richard Spilsbury

Heinemann
LIBRARY
Chicago, Illinois

Edited by Rebecca Rissman, Dan Nunn, and John-Paul Wilkins
Designed by Steve Mead
Original illustrations © Capstone Global Library Ltd 2013
Illustrations by Gary Hanna
Picture research by Ruth Blair
Production by Alison Parsons
Originated by Capstone Global Library Ltd
Printed in China

16 15 14 13 12
10 9 8 7 6 5 4 3 2 1

Library of Congress Cataloging-in-Publication Data
Spilsbury, Richard, 1963-
  Tree / Richard Spilsbury.
    p. cm.—(Look inside)
  Includes bibliographical references and index.
  ISBN 978-1-4329-7198-4 (hb)—ISBN 978-1-4329-7205-9 (pb)
1. Trees—Microbiology--Juvenile literature. 2. Microorganisms—Juvenile literature. 3. Niche (Ecology)—Juvenile literature. I. Title.

QK475.8.S75 2013
582.16—dc23

2012011822

Acknowledgments
We would like to thank the following for permission to reproduce photographs: iStockphoto pp. 24 (© Martin Pot), 25 (© Michael Pettigrew), 27 (© DAMIAN KUZDAK); Naturepl pp. 9 (© Andrew Cooper), 19 (© Ingo Arndt), 26 right (© Andy Rouse); Shutterstock pp. 5 left (© Bruce MacQueen), 5 right (© Marek CECH), 6 (© Gorilla), 7 (© lafoto), 8 (© Virunja), 11 (© D. Kucharski & K. Kucharska), 12 (© jack53), 13 (© mlorenz), 14 (© FloridaStock), 15 (© Erik Mandre), 17 (© alslutsky), 18 (© Sergey Toronto), 20 (© Mark Bridger), 21 (© peresanz), 23 (© fotosav), 26 left (© visceralimage), 28, 29 (© Smit).

Cover photograph of a may-bug grub (*Melolontha vulgaris*) reproduced with permission of Shutterstock (© fotosav).

We would like to thank Michael Bright and Diana Bentley for their invaluable help in the preparation of this book.

Every effort has been made to contact copyright holders of any material reproduced in this book. Any omissions will be rectified in subsequent printings if notice is given to the publisher.

Contents

Some words are shown in bold, **like this**. You can find out what they mean by looking in the glossary.

Among the Branches

A tree is a **habitat**. It provides different animals with food and **shelter**. Some animals live and feed mostly among the branches of a tree.

Chickadees are small, busy birds that hop along branches looking for food. They eat **insects, caterpillars**, spiders, and berries. They make **nests** and lay eggs in holes in trees.

▲ There are many different kinds of chickadee.

A honeybee flies to a tree and walks along the branches. It sucks up sweet **nectar** from flowers. Its long tongue is hollow and works like a drinking straw!

▼ This honeybee is feeding on a tree flower.

▲ Honeybee swarms contain thousands of bees.

Swarms of honeybees sometimes make **nests** on tree branches. They use nectar to make honey in the nest. They store the honey to eat in winter, when there are not many flowers around.

The gray squirrel is a **mammal** that spends most of its life up trees. It uses its strong teeth to feed on nuts and seeds. The squirrel's long, bushy tail helps it to balance as it leaps from branch to branch.

Squirrels collect food from the branches. ▶

▲ Baby squirrels huddle together to stay warm.

Female squirrels make **nests** among the branches. Baby squirrels are safe and warm in a nest. They only come out to eat nuts after their teeth have grown.

In the Trunk

Some animals live for part of the time inside a tree **trunk**. Others search for animals to eat under the **bark** of trees.

Bark beetles bite through tree bark to eat the soft wood underneath. They also lay eggs under bark. **Larvae** that **hatch** from the eggs eat the wood, too.

▲ Bark beetles eat wood from tree trunks.

Barn owls make **nests** in holes in tree **trunks**. The **female** owl sits on the eggs to keep them warm until the babies **hatch**. The **male** owl catches and brings her food.

▼ This barn owl is peering out from its nest.

▲ Barn owls fly silently.

Barn owls eat mice, frogs, and other small animals. They sit and listen for **prey** scurrying on the ground. Then they swoop down to catch it.

Woodpeckers ▶
have heavy,
pointed beaks.

Woodpeckers
peck quickly to
make holes in tree
trunks. Then they make
their **nests** inside. Adult
birds will attack owls and
other birds that try to eat eggs
or chicks from their nest.

Woodpeckers grip tree trunks using their strong **talons**. They poke their sharp beaks under the **bark** to feel for **insects** to eat. Their long, sticky tongues pick up the insects they find.

This woodpecker is ▶ feeling for insects with its tongue.

Around the Base

Some smaller animals crawl up onto trees around the base. Other larger animals stand by trees and nibble at parts of the **trunk** they can reach.

Holly blue butterflies fly around trees. **Females** lay eggs on ivy that grows up tree trunks. Green **caterpillars** then **hatch** from the eggs and eat ivy buds, berries, and leaves.

▲ Holly blue butterflies have striped **antennae**.

A ladybug is a kind of beetle. Birds eat a lot of beetles, but they usually leave ladybugs alone. Ladybugs' bright colors warn birds that they taste bad!

▼ Red and black colors are a warning signal.

Some ladybugs ▶ huddle together in cracks in tree trunks when it gets cold.

Ladybugs crawl along tree **trunks** looking for small **insects** to eat. Many ladybugs sleep in gaps under the **bark** during winter, when it is too cold to find much food.

Some deer live in woodlands. They feed on buds, leaves, nuts, and berries. In the winter, deer sometimes eat the **bark** off trees, when other food is hard to find.

▼ These deer are alert to danger.

antlers

The antlers ▶ of male deer can grow very large.

Young **males** scratch their new **antlers** against tree **trunks**. This rubs off the skin that protects the antlers while they grow. But it can damage some trees.

Among the Roots

Many animals find **shelter** and food in the ground beneath a tree. They live in the soil and dead leaves among the **roots**.

Some beetles lay their eggs in the soil among tree roots. Curled, white **larvae hatch** from the eggs and eat the roots. They grow and change into beetles.

▲ Beetle larvae eat and eat so they can grow.

Many millipedes live among tree **roots**. They mostly come out at night to chomp dead leaves. Millipedes do not see well, so they feel their way along using their **antennae**.

▼ A millipede is on the move!

antenna

▲ Millipedes come in many different colors.

Millipedes are long, thin animals with many legs. All of their little legs move quickly to help them crawl through soil. When scared, millipedes curl up tight.

Badgers often dig large holes to live in beneath tree **roots**. The roots hold up the roofs of their **dens**. They stay in the dens in the day and come out at **dusk** to feed and play.

▼ The American badger (left) and European badger (right) are slightly different colors.

▲ Badgers are shy and try to avoid humans.

Badgers use their tough claws to dig out dens and food from the soil. They have wide, flat teeth to chew worms and **larvae**. They also eat frogs, slugs, and other small animals.

Tree Habitats

Spring and summer are the seasons when many trees have leaves and flowers. Many animals visit trees because there is lots of food to eat. Most baby animals are born at this time, too.

▼ This is a tree in summer.

▲ This is a tree in winter.

In the winter, many trees lose their leaves. The branches are bare and the ground is cold. Fewer animals visit trees, and some sleep underground in **nests** and **dens**, waiting for spring to come.

Glossary

antennae (singular: antenna) thin parts on the heads of some animals, including beetles and lobsters, that are used to feel and touch

antler bony body part that grows on a male deer's head

bark tough outer covering of a tree trunk and branches

caterpillar young stage in the life cycle of a butterfly or moth

den hidden home or resting place of some animals, such as badgers or bears

dusk time of day just before night

female sex of an animal or plant that is able to produce eggs or seeds. Males are the opposite sex.

habitat place where particular types of living things are likely to live. For example, polar bears live in snowy habitats and camels live in desert habitats.

hatch come out of an egg

insect type of small animal that has three body parts, six legs, and usually wings. Ants and dragonflies are types of insect.

larvae young of some animals, such as insects

male sex of an animal or plant that is unable to produce eggs or seeds. Females are the opposite sex.

mammal animal that has hair and feeds its babies with milk from the mother. Humans and squirrels are types of mammal.

nectar sweet liquid made by flowers to attract insects and other animals

nest place where a bird or other animal lays eggs or cares for its young. Nests are often made from twigs or grass.

prey animal that is caught and eaten by another animal

root underground part of a plant that takes in water and useful substances from the soil

shelter place that provides protection from danger or bad weather

swarm large group of flying insects

talon claw of a bird

trunk part of a tree above the ground that supports the tree's branches

Find Out More

Books

Cooper, Sharon Katz. *Rotten Logs and Forest Floors* (Horrible Habitats). Chicago: Raintree, 2010.

Kalman, Bobbie. *Baby Animals in Forest Habitats* (Habitats of Baby Animals). New York: Crabtree, 2011.

Llewellyn, Claire. *Forests* (Habitat Survival). Chicago: Raintree, 2013.

Web sites

Facthound offers a safe, fun way to find web sites related to this book. All of the sites on Facthound have been researched by our staff.

Here's all you do:

Visit www.facthound.com

Type in this code: 9781432971984

Index